Learn About
Latitude and Longitude

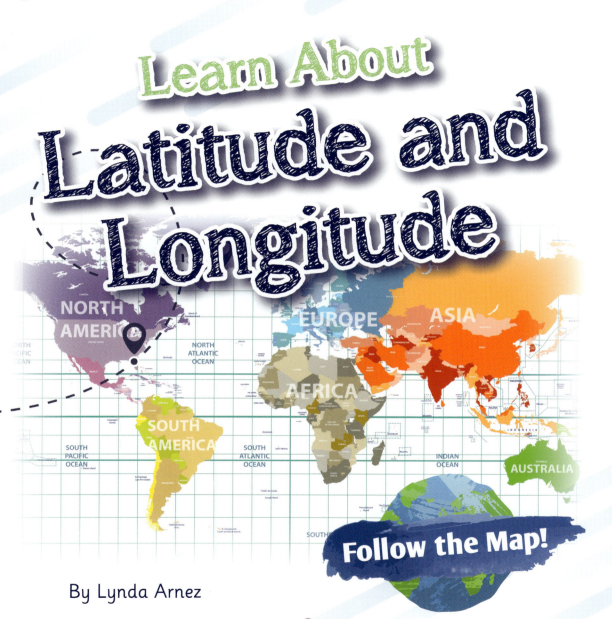

Follow the Map!

By Lynda Arnez

Enslow
PUBLISHING

Please visit our website, www.enslow.com. For a free color catalog of all our high-quality books, call toll free 1-800-398-2504 or fax 1-877-980-4454.

Library of Congress Cataloging-in-Publication Data

Names: Arnéz, Lynda, author.
Title: Learn about latitude and longitude / Lynda Arnez.
Description: Buffalo, New York : Enslow Publishing, [2024] | Series: Follow the map! | Includes bibliographical references and index. | Audience: Grades 2-3
Identifiers: LCCN 2022050455 (print) | LCCN 2022050456 (ebook) | ISBN 9781978535763 (library binding) | ISBN 9781978535756 (paperback) | ISBN 9781978535770 (ebook)
Subjects: LCSH: Latitude–Juvenile literature. | Longitude–Juvenile literature.
Classification: LCC QB224.5 .A76 2024 (print) | LCC QB224.5 (ebook) | DDC 526/.6–dc23/eng20230119
LC record available at https://lccn.loc.gov/2022050455
LC ebook record available at https://lccn.loc.gov/2022050456

Published in 2024 by
Enslow Publishing
2544 Clinton Street
Buffalo, NY 14224

Copyright © 2024 Enslow Publishing

Designer: Shelby Mammoser
Editor: Kristen Nelson

Portions of this work were originally authored by Kristen Rajczak and published as *Latitude and Longitude*. All new material in this edition authored by Lynda Arnez.

Photo credits: Cover, pp. 3, 24 (watercolor earth) Ardea-studio/Shutterstock.com; Cover, series art (map path) Pro-author/Shutterstock.com; Cover, p. 1 (latitude/longitude world map) brichuas/Shutterstock.com; p. 5 Freebird7977/Shutterstock.com; p. 7 Triff/Shutterstock.com; p. 8 Oleksandr Berezko/Shutterstock.com; p. 9 (globe) Sakurra/Shutterstock.com; p. 11 (night sky) guteksk7/Shutterstock.com; p. 11 (degree world map) pOrbital.com/Shutterstock.com; p. 13 (Galileo Galilei) Nicku/Shutterstock.com; p. 13 (latitude and longitude) EreborMountain/Shutterstock.com; p. 15 Stephen M Brooks/Shutterstock.com; p. 17 frees/Shutterstock.com; p. 19 (latitude and longitude lines of US) Rainer Lesniewski/Shutterstock.com; p. 19 (US map), 21 Fourleaflover/Shutterstock.com; p. 20 PRESSLAB/Shutterstock.com.

CPSIA compliance information: Batch #CSENS24: For further information contact Enslow Publishing at 1-800-398-2504.

Find us on

Contents

Boldface words appear in the glossary.

What's the Global Address?

How can two people who don't speak the same language give each other directions? They can use a place's "**global** address," or its **coordinates**!

The coordinates that make up a global address are on the **grid** of imaginary lines used on maps and globes. They help find a certain place on Earth. It's important for the coordinates of global addresses to be numbers because nearly everyone on Earth can understand them, no matter what language they speak.

IMAGINE TRYING TO FIND A FRIEND'S HOUSE AND NOT UNDERSTANDING HOW U.S. ADDRESSES WORK. WITH COORDINATES, YOU WOULDN'T NEED TO!

Map Basics!

Coordinates work two ways. You can use a map to find the coordinates of a certain place. Or, someone can give you coordinates of a place, and you can use a map to find it.

5

An Old Idea

The idea for a grid system for locating places started long ago. Both the ancient Greeks and Chinese tried to do it. An ancient Greek **geographer** named Ptolemy (TAHL-uh-mee) used a grid and coordinates similar to those used today to map many places.

The grid used today is made up of crossing lines of latitude and longitude. They're measured in degrees using the ° **symbol**. Coordinates made up of latitude and longitude can tell you exactly where something is on Earth.

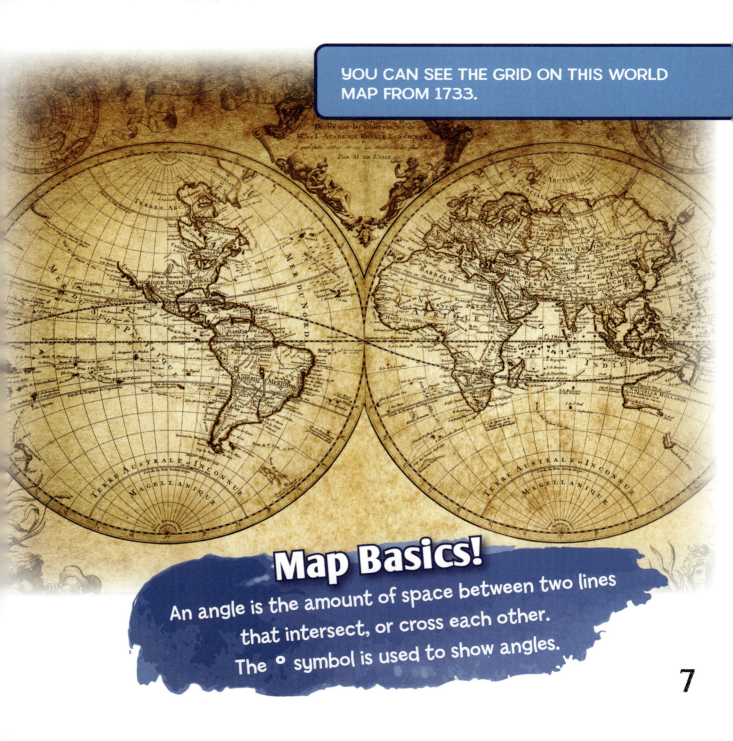

Map Basics!

An angle is the amount of space between two lines that intersect, or cross each other. The ° symbol is used to show angles.

Around the Center

The equator is 0° latitude. It is the imaginary line that runs around the center of Earth and splits it into halves. The halves are called hemispheres. The Northern Hemisphere is above the equator. The Southern Hemisphere is below the equator. Every part of the equator is equally **distant** from the North Pole and the South Pole.

The equator is the most important line of latitude. It is the line of latitude upon which all the other latitude lines are based.

THE EQUATOR IS THE LONGEST LINE OF LATITUDE. IT'S 24,901.55 MILES (40,075.2 KM) LONG AND RUNS THROUGH COLOMBIA AND KENYA, AS WELL AS OTHER COUNTRIES.

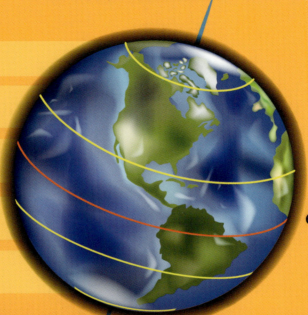

equator (0° latitude)

Map Basics!

Even early maps had the equator on them. Early people used the sun to find location, and it's the place on Earth that gets the most sun.

Running Parallel

Lines of latitude are called parallels. They run parallel to each other, or are the same distance apart and never touch along their whole length. They run east and west above and below the equator. They show how far north or south a place is.

Latitude coordinates fall between 0° and 90°. They're a measurement of the angle created when you draw a line from the center of Earth to the equator and a line from the center of Earth to the parallel.

THE HIGHER THE NUMBER OF A PARALLEL'S COORDINATE, THE FARTHER IT IS FROM THE EQUATOR.

North Pole (+)

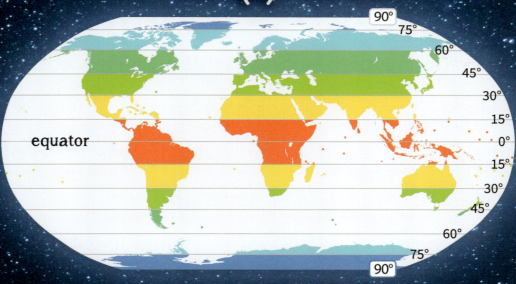

equator

North Pole (+)

90°
75°
60°
45°
30°
15°
0°
15°
30°
45°
60°
75°
90°

South Pole (–)

Map Basics!

A northern parallel has a latitude coordinate with a plus sign (+) before it or "N" after it. A southern parallel has a latitude coordinate with a minus sign (–) before it or "S" after it.

Looking for Longitude

The other number that makes up a place's coordinates is longitude. Longitude shows how far east or west a place is. In the 1600s, Galileo measured longitude using a ship's local time and the time at its home **port**.

Earth completes its full 360° **rotation** in 24 hours. That means a given point on the planet moves 15° of longitude each hour. The difference between local time and the time at a ship's home port showed how many degrees of longitude a ship had traveled.

BECAUSE OF HOW EARTH IS SHAPED, LINES OF LONGITUDE ARE ALL THE SAME LENGTH. LINES OF LATITUDE ARE NOT.

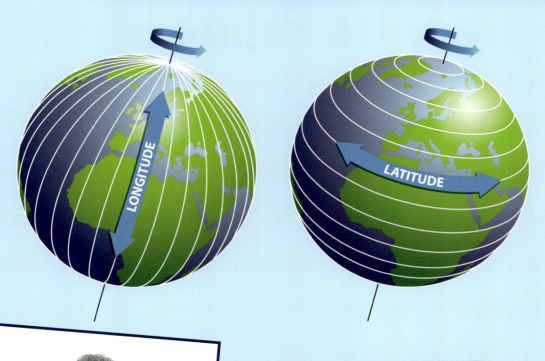

LONGITUDE

LATITUDE

Galileo Galilei.

Map Basics!

Galileo Galilei was an Italian scientist who used the moons of Jupiter to figure out how to measure longitude at sea!

It's Prime

Another imaginary line drawn around Earth's center runs north-south! It's called the prime meridian. It splits Earth into the Eastern and Western Hemispheres. In 1884, a group of nations set the prime meridian as the longitude line that passes through Greenwich, England. The prime meridian is 0° longitude.

Lines of longitude are called meridians. That's because they run to the east and west of the prime meridian. Meridians run from the North Pole to the South Pole.

Latitud:
38º 51' 58'' N
Longitud:
0º 0' 0,00''

Meridià de Greenwich

Map Basics!

Meridians are measured in degrees that range from 0° to 180°.

More About Longitude

Lines of longitude east of the prime meridian are written with a plus sign (+) before them or "E" after them. Lines of longitude west of the prime meridian are written with a minus sign (–) before them or "W" after them.

At 180° longitude lies the international date line. This is the longitude line chosen to mark the place where each calendar day begins. It is halfway around the world from the prime meridian! The international date line only runs through the ocean, not any countries.

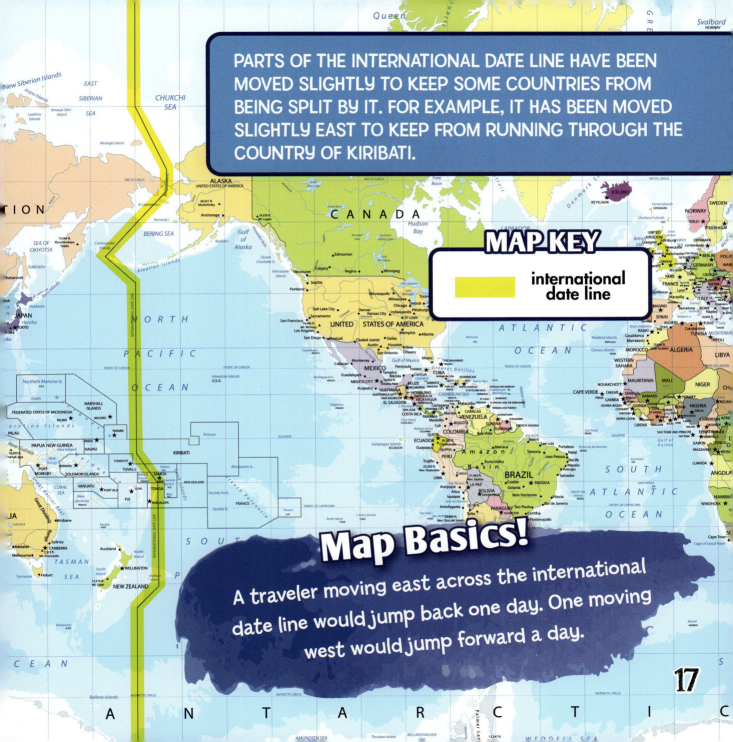

PARTS OF THE INTERNATIONAL DATE LINE HAVE BEEN MOVED SLIGHTLY TO KEEP SOME COUNTRIES FROM BEING SPLIT BY IT. FOR EXAMPLE, IT HAS BEEN MOVED SLIGHTLY EAST TO KEEP FROM RUNNING THROUGH THE COUNTRY OF KIRIBATI.

MAP KEY

international date line

Map Basics!

A traveler moving east across the international date line would jump back one day. One moving west would jump forward a day.

17

Breaking It Down

The latitude and longitude measurements are both needed to give a location. The intersection of those lines can tell you exactly where you are on Earth or on a map! When writing coordinates, the latitude measurement comes first.

Degrees of latitude and longitude are broken down into smaller units of minutes and seconds. They show just how close to a meridian or parallel a place is. There are 60 minutes in each degree. There are 60 seconds in each minute.

THIS MAP OF THE UNITED STATES HAS LATITUDE LINES RUNNING FROM LEFT TO RIGHT AND LONGITUDE LINES RUNNING FROM TOP TO BOTTOM. ON EACH LINE IS A NUMBER. THAT'S THE MEASUREMENT OF THE PARALLEL OR MERIDIAN IN DEGREES.

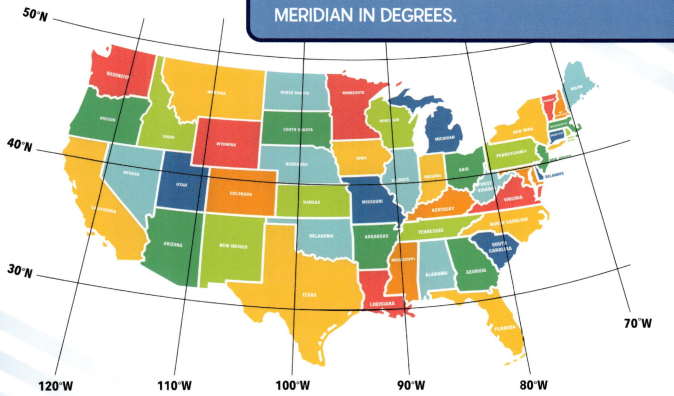

Map Basics!

Minutes are shown by the symbol ' and seconds are shown by ".

19

Coordinates Today

Understanding coordinates is just as important today as it ever was! They can be helpful if your family is driving or biking through a park or the mountains, or boating down a river.

Did you know that you can put latitude and longitude coordinates into a GPS? Many people carry around smartphones with mapping **apps** in their pocket. With coordinates, you have the most **accurate** way of telling where something is!

THOSE WHO ENJOY GEOCACHING USE THE INTERNET TO FIND SETS OF COORDINATES. THEY FOLLOW A MAP OR GPS TO THE SPOT AND FIND NOTES, OBJECTS, OR TREASURES OTHER GEOCACHERS HAVE LEFT BEHIND.

Find U.S. Cities!

CHECK OUT THE COORDINATES OF MAJOR CITIES IN THE UNITED STATES!

Seattle, Washington
47° 36' 28.8468" N
122° 20' 6.6012" W

Kansas City, Missouri
39° 5' 59.0064" N
94° 34' 41.9916" W

New York, New York
40° 43' 50.1960" N
73° 56' 6.8712" W

Los Angeles, California
34° 3' 8.0460" N
118° 14' 37.2588" W

Dallas, Texas
32° 46' 45.0012" N
96° 48' 32.0076" W

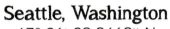

Map Basics!

GPS stands for global positioning system. This system uses **satellite** signals to locate places on Earth.

21

Glossary

accurate: Free from error.

app: Short for application, a computer or smartphone program that has a certain function.

coordinate: Any of a set of numbers used in specifying the location of a point on a line, on a plane, or in space.

distant: Far off.

geographer: A person who studies geography, or the study of Earth's natural features.

global: Having to do with the whole world.

grid: A set of squares formed by crisscrossing lines.

port: A place, like a town or city, where ships stop to load and unload cargo.

rotation: The act of turning.

satellite: An object that circles Earth in order to collect and send information or aid in communication.

symbol: A picture, shape, or object that stands for something else.

For More Information

Books

Aschim, Hans. *How to Go Anywhere (and Not Get Lost): A Guide to Navigation for Young Adventurers.* New York, NY: Workman Publishing, 2021.

Beginner's World Atlas. Washington, DC: National Geographic Kids, 2022.

Websites

ABCya! Latitude and Longitude Game

www.abcya.com/latitude_and_longitude_practice.htm
Hunt for treasure and practice your map skills at the same time with this game.

What Is Geocaching?

www.wonderopolis.org/wonder/what-is-geocaching
Find out more about geocaching here.

INDEX